In a wood next to a big river, there lived a fox and a stork. One morning, they met on the bank of the river.
   "Come and have some dinner with me," said the fox to the stork, "Yes, thank you, I will," replied the stork.

In ɐ wood next to ɐ big river, theer lived ɐ fox and ɐ stork. Wun morning, thay met on the baŋk ov the river.
   "Cume and have sume dinner with me," sed the fox to the stork, "Yes, thaŋk you, Ie will," replied the stork.

So the fox set about cooking dinner. He mixed, cut, chopped and added until he had made a big pot of food.
"Mmmm, that smells good," said the fox. He looked into the pot and licked his lips.

So the fox set ebout cooking dinner. He mixed, cut, chopped and addid until he had made e big pot ov food.
"Mmmm, that smells good," sed the fox. He looked into the pot and licked his lips.

When the stork arrived, she said, "Mmmm, that smells good. I did not catch much fish this morning, so I am very hungry."

When the stork errievd, she sed, "Mmmm, that smells good. Ie did not catch much fish this morning, so Ie am vere hungre."

The fox and the stork sat down to dinner. The fox spooned out the food onto the big flat plates he had set out.

The fox and the stork sat doun to dinner. The fox spooned out the food onto the big flat plates he had set out.

The stork pecked at the food with her long pointed bill, but it was hard for her as the plate was so flat. She pecked and pecked but she only ate a little of her food.

The stork pecked at the food with her long pointid bill, but it wos hard for her as the plate wos so flat. She pecked and pecked but she onle ate e littel ov her food.

When he had finished his dinner, the fox licked his lips. "Mmmm, that was good," he said. "Have you finished?" he added, looking at the stork's plate.

"My bill is too long and pointed for this big flat plate," the stork explained. She was still very hungry, and it made her angry when the fox quickly ate all the food she had left as well.

When he had finished his dinner, the fox licked his lips. "Mmmm, that wos good," he sed. "Have you finished?" he addid, looking at the stork's plate.

"My bill is too long and pointid for this big flat plate," the stork explained . She wos still vere hungre, and it made her angre when the fox quickle ate all the food she had left as well.

When the fox came to the river bank next week, he found the stork there, waiting for him.

"Will you come and have dinner with me this evening?" she said.

"Yes, thank you, I will," said the fox, licking his lips greedily.

"I am so glad," said the stork politely, but she smiled to herself.

When the fox came to the river bank next week, he found the stork theer, waiting for him.

"Will you cume and have dinner with me this evening?" she sed.

"Yes, thank you, Ie will," sed the fox, licking his lips greedile.

"Ie am so glad," sed the stork polietle, but she smield to herself.

This time, it was the stork who cooked the dinner. She mixed, cut, chopped and added until she had made a big pot of food.

"Mmmm," the stork said to herself. "That smells good."

This tiem, it wos the stork who cooked the dinner. She mixed, cut, chopped and addid until she had made e big pot ov food.

"Mmmm," the stork sed to herself. "That smells good."

When the fox arrived, he sniffed the food cooking.
"Mmmm," he said, "that smells good. I am hungry," and he rubbed his belly.

When the fox errievd, he sniffed the food cooking.
"Mmmm," he sed, "that smells good. Ie am hungre," and he rubbed his belle.

The stork and the fox sat down to dinner. The stork spooned out the food into the tall thin jars she had set out.

The stork and the fox sat doun to dinner. The stork spooned out the food into the tall thin jars she had set out.

The fox tried to lick his food out of the top of the jar, but it was hard for him as the jar was so tall and thin. He licked and licked but he only ate a little of his food.

The fox tried to lick his food out ov the top ov the jar, but it wos hard for him as the jar wos so tall and thin. He licked and licked but he onle ate e littel ov his food.

He had to sit and see the stork peck up all her dinner with her long thin bill. "Mmmm. That was good," she said.

"Have you finished?" she said, looking at all the food the fox had left.

"I cannot lick more. This jar is too tall and thin for me," he explained.

He had to sit and see the stork peck up all her dinner with her long thin bill. "Mmmm. That wos good," she sed.

"Have you finished?" she sed, looking at all the food the fox had left.

"Ie cannot lick more. This jar is too tall and thin for me," he explained.

The greedy fox was angry when the stork finished up the rest of the food in his jar. He still felt hungry as he had had so little dinner.

The greede fox wos angre when the stork finished up the rest ov the food in his jar. He still felt hungre as he had had so littel dinner.

"Well," the stork said, "I was upset when I came to dinner with you, and you gave me a big flat plate."

"I am sorry," the fox said. "It was wrong of me. Come and have dinner with me again next week, and this time will be different."

"Well," the stork sed, "Ie wos upset when Ie came to dinner with you, and you gave me e big flat plate."

"Ie am sorre," the fox sed. "It wos wrong ov me. Cume and have dinner with me egain next week, and this tiem will be different."

So next week, the stork went to have dinner with the fox again. Before she arrived, the fox chopped, cut, added and mixed, until he had a big pot of food.

"Mmmm, that smells good," he said.

So next week, the stork went to have dinner with the fox again. Before she arrievd, the fox chopped, cut, addid and mixed, until he had e big pot ov food.

"Mmmm, that smells good," he sed.

When the stork arrived, she smiled and said, "That smells good."

"Thank you. Come and sit down," said the fox.

He set out a big flat plate for himself again, but he gave the stork a tall thin jar. This time she had no problem getting at her food, and she ate plenty!

When the stork errievd, she smield and sed, "That smells good."

"Thank you. Cume and sit doun," sed the fox.

He set out e big flat plate for himself egain, but he gave the stork e tall thin jar. This tiem she had no problem getting at her food, and she ate plente!